yellow

25.64

MAGIC CASTLE READERS®

Nanny Goat's Boat

A book of rhyming

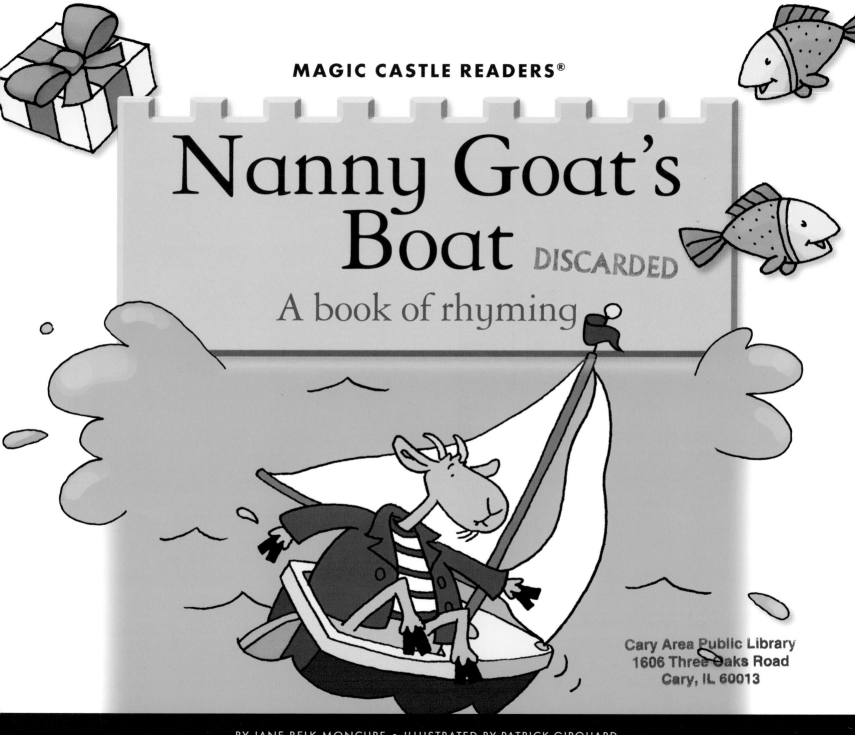

BY JANE BELK MONCURE • ILLUSTRATED BY PATRICK GIROUARD

The Child's World

Published by The Child's World®
1980 Lookout Drive • Mankato, MN 56003-1705
800-599-READ • www.childsworld.com

Acknowledgments
The Child's World®: Mary Berendes, Publishing Director
The Design Lab: Design
Jody Jensen Shaffer: Editing

ISBN 9781623235673
LCCN 2013931408

Printed in the United States of America
Mankato, MN
July 2013
PA02177

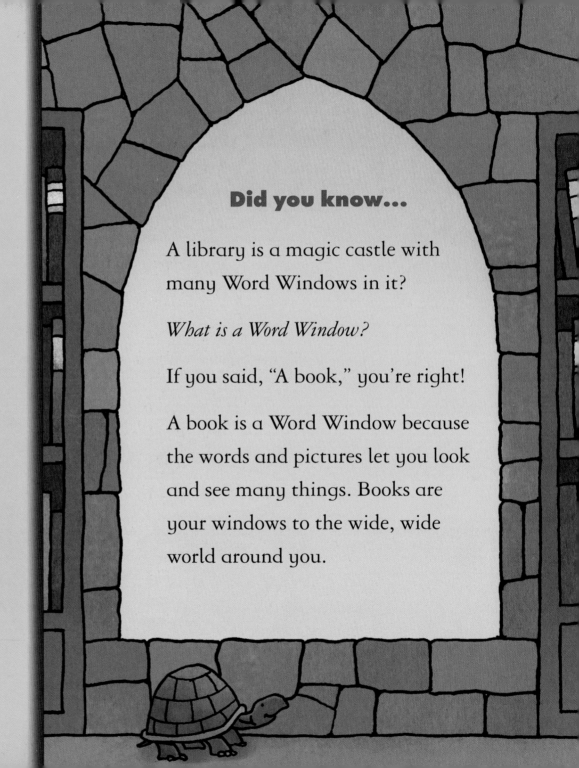

Did you know...

A library is a magic castle with many Word Windows in it?

What is a Word Window?

If you said, "A book," you're right!

A book is a Word Window because the words and pictures let you look and see many things. Books are your windows to the wide, wide world around you.

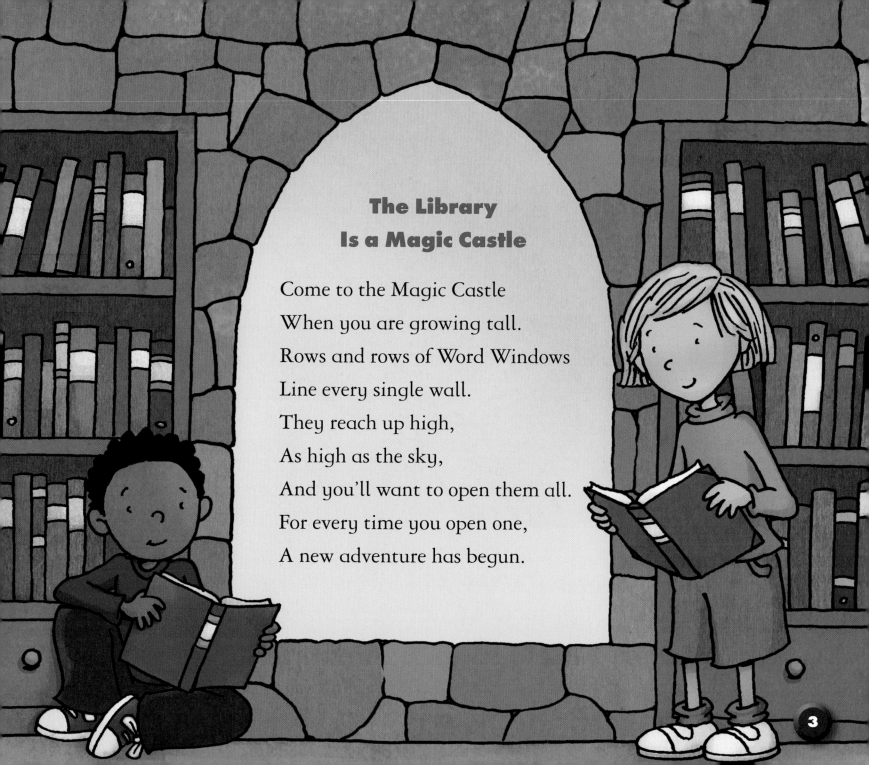

The Library Is a Magic Castle

Come to the Magic Castle
When you are growing tall.
Rows and rows of Word Windows
Line every single wall.
They reach up high,
As high as the sky,
And you'll want to open them all.
For every time you open one,
A new adventure has begun.

Sam opened a Word Window.
Here is what he read:

Nanny Goat had a boat.
It was a little sailboat.

"I will sail away," she said one day.

But the boat would not float.
Then Nanny Goat lost her coat.

She was wet from her nose
to the tips of her toes.

Nanny Goat soon had a sore throat.
She went to the doctor. Guess what he said.
"Drink some soup and stay in bed."

Goat's friends came to visit, one at a time.
To cheer her up, each one came with a rhyme.

Fox said, "Guess what is in this box.
Is it a tie or two pairs of socks?"

Nanny Goat said,
"Socks. Thank you, Fox."

Cat came with something in a hat.
"Is it a bird or a ball and a bat?"

Nanny Goat said, "A ball and a bat.
Thank you, Cat!"

Three butterflies came with a sweet surprise.
"Close your eyes," said the butterflies.
"Is this a book or a strawberry pie?"

Nanny Goat said, "Pie.
Thank you, butterflies!"

Two kangaroos jumped up the stairs.
"We brought you things that come in pairs."

"Two pairs of gloves, or two pairs of shoes.
Can you guess?" asked the kangaroos.

Nanny Goat did. Can you?

Ape came with a gift for Nanny Goat.
"This is to wear when you sail in your boat."

"Is it a scarf or a cap?" asked the ape.
You know! Isn't that so?

Bear also gave Nanny Goat something to wear.
"Is it a dress or a bow for your hair?" asked Bear.

Did Nanny Goat say, "A bow for my hair, Bear"?

Bunny gave Nanny Goat something funny.
"Is this a balloon or a bank full of money?"
asked Bunny.

"Great!" said Nanny Goat.
"I can buy a new boat."
She quickly got over her bad sore throat.

Then Nanny Goat bought a new boat.

The new boat could float!

Nanny Goat wrote each friend a little note:

Thank you for rhyming me a rhyme.
Come sailing with me anytime.
You have been so nice to me.
Come to my party
At half past three!

So Goat is giving a party. My, what a treat!
Guess what. There is one empty seat.
The seat is for you!

Goat says, "Rhyme me a rhyme,
and come to my party anytime!"

Questions and Activities

(Write your answers on a sheet of paper.)

1. Describe Nanny Goat. Write two things about her.

2. How did Nanny Goat end up in the water?
   Why is Nanny Goat sick in bed after she falls in the water?

3. Look at the picture on page 27. What does it tell about how Nanny Goat feels about her new boat?

4. What does it mean when Nanny Goat says, "Rhyme me a rhyme"? How do you know it means that?

5. Tell this story to a friend. Take only two minutes. Which parts did you share?